# Poetry
## Manifest

by Philip Finkle

authorHOUSE®

*AuthorHouse™*
*1663 Liberty Drive*
*Bloomington, IN 47403*
*www.authorhouse.com*
*Phone: 1 (800) 839-8640*

*Published by AuthorHouse 08/27/2015*

*ISBN: 978-1-5049-2545-7 (sc)*
*ISBN: 978-1-5049-2544-0 (e)*

*Library of Congress Control Number: 2015912036*

*Print information available on the last page.*

Part One:

DOUBTS AND REDOUBTS

"It is on disaster that good fortune perches;
It is beneath good fortune that disaster crouches."

- Tao Te Ching

## DOUBTS AND REDOUBTS

# UNPOEM

An unpoem has
  no rhyme
       nor reason ore
any grammar either
        or it wouldn't be
                  one, un
          that it Its
        .punctuation
            don't help anything
                        can be a mess but
              only a lot of things
        Are unpoems
                  or are they or us
                          either
          Every thing and everybody may
              somehow be a poem
                  someday rather than
                      an unpoem?

                    (1971)

# DAYBREAK

At the dawning of our new daze all of the middleminds were shuffling their fats and indexing their little cardthoughts.

Technical waves washed the shore white, lily-white, death-white, gone-white,

And tubers sprouted in the arid sands of deserted lands of pallid ancestry.

Rulers of past heraldry dryly doffed hats of crimsom to tarnished ladies.

And the winds howled: the humming winds of desolate things,

While miserly maidens picked sad blooms from the misery bush and empty hands grasped the morning's throat.

Mourning doves wobbled through thoughtless forests in search of good deeds for the rejected trees.


And yet the sprouts of Burlington and Buena Vista waved their tattered pennants in hope of due penance,

For all of the teary ones had since long departed to relatives of the storm,

And orphans adrift were aparted, alerted by the cries of
    dying beeches and able spruces of warlock pride.

The enchanted woodlands, being spritely attired, retried
    returning wards.

Hordes of the sickcast beached ahead on the palsied
    shoreline, trailing smoke thoughts.

And yet, and yet, our words grew dim and he who wasted
    wanted not,

For tiny knots and clusters of starshapes had accrued in
    the abscence of misdeeds,

And strong steeds galloped past the rising sons of Sun's
    house in skies of glory,

And the purple haze of done victories retreated before the
    bright clawing of forgiveness.

Redress of addled dreams seems softly now,

And we must come together.

    And we must come together.

(1972)

# IN MY PRIME

From off the top it came one night
"You're in your prime,"

she said.

She meant to speak of lusty things
she did

I heard

I hid.

Just old enough to know something
Yet young enough to use it

Compelled enough to risk it all
Resolved enough to lose it.

In my prime –

that's in my time,

not of it.

Before design,

after my crime

but not above it.

I came on stage

clothed in just words,

post-entrance

and pre-exit.

"I'll repeat this only once,"

I said,

resplendent

and redundant.

And then I breathed

and lunged

and heaved

and shoved myself

r i g h t

past me.

"where am i now?"

I asked

she smiled

I knew

I'd passed it.

(1972)

# MONEY TALKS

Money talks.

It says,

> "Money is power, pal –
> > Show me a featherless biped
> > > and I'll show you an easy mark."

It says,

> "Kick your shoes off, cousin,
> Put your feet up,
> Let me make you a deal you Can't refuse,
> I mean *thou shalt not reject* this offer, pilgrim!
> > "Peddle your cratered soul for
> > > a half-a-dream's worth of synapse juice!
> > > > (You central-nervous-system-types
> > > > > tend strongly to the tyrannical.)"

It says,

> "You want to see something sister?
> I'm talking the grease the squeaky one gets,
> The brew the bankers stir,

The veritable lubricious pelf that powers the drummer,
The specie that soothes the whir of the gears of com-
merce."

It says,
    "This wealth shines brightly, buster,
    Fueled by the flames of burning 'fossil-love' –
    'Fossil-love' sapped by the drills of the
                        power-suckers,
                        power-liners,
                        main-liners,
                        hard-liners,
    and possibly-just-a-few-lines-left-creatures
    slouching towards the Southgate Shopping Mall."

Money talks.
    It doesn't listen.
        It never learns –
            "'Power as a gift of the life force',
                Use it wisely little pennymonger,
                    For there are bigger things a-brew,
                        Yes, far bigger things than you."

                                            (1980)

# GONER'S RAG

what you gonna do when the fire starts?
  what you gonna do when its flamin'?
when you call for help my friend,
  who you gonna be namin'?

where you gonna keep your valuables, ma'm,
  Through lightning and through thunder?
who gonna help you rise above?
  what gonna drag you under?

How you gonna pay when the man collects?
  what's it take to buy you?
where you gonna keep the things you know
  when the things you don't fly by you?

what you gonna use to fight off lions?
  what to scare the danger?
what colors will you finally fly,
  when you meet that last sad stranger?

(1982)

# REPORT TO THE FISHERMAN

It was the fattest of times,
                    It was the leanest of times.
    It was the serenest of times,
                        It was the meanest of times.
For the Few there was more of the Bounty
    For the Many there was less of the Plenty.
El Dorado lay down with the Sheik's concubines
    and woke up hungry.
Their gods were of metal and fire,
        and they worshipped them
                        to the point of exhaustion:
            A selfish, short-sighted, hedonistic,
                    hell-bent-for-leather group
                            barreling   down   the
cut-off to Hell,
        no exit,
    no deposit,
no return,
no shit.
            O arrogance of power,
                crash of great opulent towers,

rotted at the cores,

whores of power politics

and executions in the night.

Ah, the flickering lights of Gehenna:

How inviting;

But here,

another automobile-orphan,

and there,

    another war-orphan,

Lord,

    there are so many.

"Only the young die good,"

    the torturer said.


What comes after?

    what restores laughter?

      we don't need a revolution.

        we need a reconstitution of values –

        of course

          that will probably take a revolution.

(1984)

# TO A MOUNTAIN BARTENDER

The juncos have arrived
    with the conviction of winter.
 They chatter of Canadian adventures
    while Northern storms track them to the
                     Colorado Rockies.
This is a proper time for dust
                to rejoin dust –
 Before the stare of death
    freezes to sheer ice.
 whatever part of you can escape
    will slowly accrue to the landscape.
    Your gesture now will be
      the flicker of the yellowing aspen
        and the wave of long mountain grasses:
          Death being graduation
            to a voiceless realm.
So let us hoist a glass
    in the presence of our final host –
 that dark silent stranger at the end of the bar,
               naturally.
    we cannot discern his shrouded features.

It's as if he stands in a mist.

Yet

Here's to the one who served the brew

that helps us momentarily forget

that last appointment we must keep.

"Bartender!

Drinks all 'round!"

(1987, Idaho Springs, Colorado)

# MEDICINE TALE

Kiowa woman –
　　you have stepped outside the hoop.
　　　　Did you trade all of your ponies
　　　　　　　　　　　　for this pick-up?
　　　　What are you searching for
　　　　　　　　　　here in the white man's city?
　　　　　　Was your grandfather not pulled under
　　　　　　　　　　　　the Whiskey River?
　　　　　　　　And now there are many more drugs to
enchain you.
　　　　　　The forces of decadence crave meat and metal.
　　　　　Occasional presents become permanent pasts
　　　　　　　　　　　　(love seldom lasts).
　　　　　　　Market-wise and profoundly ghoulish,
　　　　　　Every nightrider wants to touch your magic.
　　　　　　　Now you've learned the steps
　　　　　　　　　　but the steps have changed:
　　　　　　　　　　　　The dance you're mastered
　　has been rearranged.
　　In crazy dreams of modern robot romance, here we
come again:

always extremist in pursuit of profit or pleasure –
we lie entwined like exhausted contestants
    for the title of "world's Greatest Consumer",
        while some realist explains,
            "Money's thicker than love,
                words more slippery than blood."
And you can't throw fastballs all day long,
    Though the covetous chorus sings,
        "we want roses for nothing."
All of the best thoughts have been thought,
    But few actions have been taken.
Though no promises were made,
        All the best words have been spoken.
    All of the smoke's best intentions
        Are but the fire's trail of desire.
Wealthy scavengers eye the earth-jugular,
    while owl-priests grow restless
                in the shrinking jungles.
        So *bruja* to *brujo* –
            let us compare half-breed views:
        what future-tense-species
            awaits a word from your lips?
                (You can't trick the trickster.)
                who will plant the circle?
    All of the warriors have become worriers:
        what's a man to do?

In the present realm

   ownership is the ultimate illu-

sion.

   In the kingdom we dreamed of,

      humans had the unfenced beauty and endurance

                  of yarrow, goldenrod,

               Indian paintbrush,

                     musk thistle. . . . .

once loveless as a prime number,

      Now you have flesh like a feral logarithm

               and eyes eloquent as a corpse.

                              (1988)

# IN THE LAND OF THE ONE-EYEDS

Blesséd are the blind.

Half-blessed are we.

we've had Plenty for free.

Here,

gangsters are heroes while the humble are despised.

we chase the easy buck,

Hoping for the lottery-millionaire's luck;

or searching for that roller-coaster fuck –

a hit of the good stuff,

the big thrill and a cheap giggle.

Commerce and fashion are our truest passions.

Our new Golden Rule:

Always stimulate demand;

Always demand stimulation.

we build such elaborately beautiful theories,

which we then drive aground on such ordi-nary rocks.

For us,

the stars,

like aged hookers,

forced to hang out under the glare of sodium
vapor lamps,

       at the corner of Desperado and Seven-
teenth

           are poems painted on black velvet.


The One-Eyeds forgot
  that the Holy Goof must first be holy

         and only secondarily goofy.
But still

    there was the smell of sweetgrass burning

    and the sound of songs of human yearning –
The Lesser of Two Evils

        sashayed its finest stuff

    Past the Law of Diminishing returns.

   Being fitted for a straitjacket is a snap!
Man pontificates'

    Woman proliferates –

      Ceremony is the harvest of structure.

  Those Old-Timers who paired for once,

    together for alltime in a long slow desire,

      Admired eagles and others of their
feather:

    Together through the thin and the thick,

      Even unto death,

        slow or quick.

All these afflictions of the heart

are just rehearsals

for that final dance of departure. . .

The arrow covets the archer.

(1994)

# SHE WAS A PIRATE IN AN AGE OF SHIPWRECK

The first time I met her was in the Chinaman's kitchen.

She sipped golden seal and mushroom soup.

She chants, she encants –

"Do everything a little,

Don't do anything a lot."

There she stood determined,

one-directional like time;

reckless like history –

not like mystery:

multidirectional.

what sort of music does a savage beast make?

"Males do best as birds (think plumage).

They're most effective *en masse* (as witness armies and sperm).

For a while she lived with some starving autist,

mostly as a weight-loss scheme

and a chance to do a little modelling –

Her indiscretion grew up to become her glory.

She became mastress of the herbal heal.

She always had some kif to share,

with which to weave a wondrous spell

to lift one from the depths of hell

or just relieve a minor pain,

and there's the bind:

Blind and mindless is the curse that binds.

Where do you put the money in??

Where does the music come out?

She once ran a game in the carny;

She used to sing in the bars.

She knew when to keep her mouth shut;

She drove someone else's car.

Her life was a fiction,

like sex without friction.

worked herself into a trick groove,

demimonde of a crafty art.

She went out to comfort an old flame and got
burned:

charged with felony-possession of a vegetable.

She did some time

and now there she stands without a man,

Soon to lose her electric kid,

wearing his mystic earring and
transcendental hair:

Video-Emperor of the Mall,

A rune, a glyph, a symbol, a myth.

Too old to die young;

too scarred to live dumb.

"Yes, your uniform of dust is quite fetching,

                              far   from   the   smell   of
institutional food."

The last time I saw her was in some corner cafe.

Her every laugh ended in a cough –

She's seen enough.

She had suicide-eyes that bind

and a tight-lipped smile that unwinds like a bro-
ken watch.

she quaffs the last of her *yerba maté*.

It's Daylight's-Savings-Time-Eve

and later than you think.

(1996)

# UNREQUITED REQUISITE

"The same sun that brings out the snake,
brings out the lily."

- Uncle Joe Cannon

We're telling each other our same old stories again,
        but in their latest versions.
        (I worked on the railroad, you soared on the great
winds.)
    You're lecturing me again on the nature of sand (life's
or love's).
        "Get a fix on it and it shifts."
    I sermonize on time's relentless flow:
        "when we end, it lifts."
    I'm only a jr. assistant weasel –
        Just another sorry cipher in some mean-
ingless capitalist scheme.
        My excuse?
        Hey, it ain't no life, but its a living.
        Fast cars and easy money.
    I've got no home page and I'm lost out on the
highway –

Because I owe the government some money for
breaking a rule

And because I owe the government some
money for obeying a rule.

You're but a bit of flesh.

I'm but a short rush of air.

I'm a piece of meat that sings.

You're the short-order cook for my grilled-
cheese life.

where there is no right there things go wrong.

where all is fright there can be no song –

A movie star with a transmissable disease,

A meditator without ease.

I can't get you out of my dreams.

I can't get you into my life.

I'm not ready to die. I'm not finished with flesh.

Oh, all the many saints of India – Rise Up!

we know more than the past

but less than the future.

(1997)

# CONTEXTS/YOUTH

### Drumbeat 1

In 1945 Ho Chi Minh declared Vietnam's independence from its French colonialist rulers. Two and one half billion dollars of U.S. aid did nothing to forestall the overwhelming of French forces by the Viet Minh in 1954 at Dien Bien Phu. The resulting Geneva Peace Conference provisionally divided Vietnam into north and south, to be reunited by an election in 1956. It was common knowledge that in a free and open election Ho Chi Minh would win in a landslide. President Eisenhower refused to allow the election and threw support to the puppet Saigon regime of Ngo Dinh Diem, a Catholic in a Buddhist country. Near the end of 1959 there were 760 "military advisors" to the 243,000 South Vietnamese Armed Forces. A Viet Cong attack on Bien Hoa brought the first two U.S. military casualities of the war.

### Interlude 1

Ten days after the French surrender at Dien Bien Phu, Thurgood Marshall's victory was handed down by the Supreme Court in Brown vs. Board of Education, calling for the racial integration of public schools.

In 1957 Elizabeth Eckford of the "Little Rock Nine" marched through a sea of white faces contorted by hatred and hurling curses and at the end of the day at Little Rock High School she returned home to wring the spit from her dress.

Automobile-empowered Neal Cassidy sped down the twisting American highway spieling his head-bobbing, hipster bop beat jive stoned "Go!" monologue – tapping time to radio, windshield wiper, tire-hum rhythm.

Black folks had the music, white folks had the money. In Memphis, Tennessee, Sam Phillips found a pretty white boy who "sounded black" when he sang – let the rock 'n roll adolescent marketing begin!

The mass-marketing of birth control pills liberated women from biological determinism; separating sex from reproduction and pleasure from consequence.

Puritanical censorship tried to muffle D.H. Lawrence, James Joyce, Henry Miller, J.D. Salinger and dropped plums in the laps of Lenny Bruce and Hugh Hefner.

Sputnik spooked us!

The Cold War-conceived Interstate Highway System increased fossil fuel consumption, further bled the railroads, metastisized suburban sprawl, sliced through ancient animal migratory routes, helped homogenize popular culture and promoted transportation by personal vehicle.

Allen Ginsburg cruised the streets of revolutionary Havana, startling *los barbudos* – the revolution for individual freedom meets the socio-economic revolution.

Television adds to the uniformity of pop culture and leads to the truest American art-form: the TV commercial, and to the explosion of celebrity-culture.

## Drumbeat 2

In January 1961, John F. Kennedy took office with 900 U.S. military personnel in Vietnam. In 1963 American television viewers were subjected to the sight of self-immolation by Buddhist monks protesting their treatment by Diem's regime. Disagreement over conduct of the war also contributed to the CIA's concurrence in the assasination of Diem in a military coup. Three weeks after Diem's assasination came Kennedy's: it was November 1963 and there were 16,300 American troops in Vietnam. In August 1964 Kennedy's successor, Lyndon Johnson distorted the Gulf of Tonkin incident into a major attack on U.S. naval vessels, requiring retaliation. In the ensuing Naval air attacks North Vietnamese forces shot down two Navy aircraft and took their first American P.O.W. when Johnson was hounded from office in 1968 U.S. troop strength stood at 536,000 – 30,600 had been killed in action.

## Interlude 2

Rosa Parks refused to give up her seat on the bus; Martin Luther King Jr. led the Montgomery bus boycott.

In 1963 in Bull Connor's Birmingham, segregationists blew up four young girls in their Bible class.

In 1964 (as the Gulf of Tonkin escalation was going on) the FBI, after a long search, dug the bodies of Andrew Goodman, James Chaney and Michael Schwerner out of an earthen dam in Mississippi. They'd traveled there to help register black voters which the Ku Klux Klan had judged punishable by torture and death.

In "bourgeois-retirement-Florida" it's "Good night, Dr. Sax"....at 47, Jack Kerouac, King of the Beats, died a raging alcoholic death.

Cassius Clay became Muhammed Ali; Dylan went electric and turned the Beatles on to pot; Timothy Leary hopscotched the country's campuses preaching his LSD-gospel of "Turn On, Tune In, Drop Out."

A sequined, bloated, Vegas-Elvis turned on to a different tune and dropped out at age 42. The King is dead.

Youth culture proved a philosophical bust but a great commercial success.

Covert chickens roosting: Patrice Lumumba assasinated in the Congo – Democratically ruling Iranian Prime Minister Mohammad Mossadeq toppled, resulting in the installation of the shah – 1954 CIA operation in Guatamela results in the overthrow of democratically elected Jacobo Arbenz – In 1967, Che Guevara, revolutionary icon, tracked down with CIA technology, captured by Bolivian forces, executed, trophy hands cut off, body hidden – with U.S. encouragement in 1973, democratically elected Chilean President Salvador Allende overthrown by the military with numerous leftists tortured, killed, disappeared.

Television brought the nobility of the civil rights struggle and the horrors of Vietnam into American livingrooms.

In 1968, in Memphis, Tennessee Martin Luther King Jr., apostle of non-violence was gunned down by the forces of hate.

Drumbeat 3

In 1969 Richard Nixon took office; by June U.S. troop strength peaked at 543,000. The policy of "Viet-namization of the war" was replacing GI's with ARVIN troops.

Inten-sive bombing of Laos and Cambodia was kept secret and then justified as disrupting supply lines along the Ho Chi Minh trail. The military's image was further degraded by the public exposure of the My Lai massacre. Ho Chi Minh died in 1969. In 1970 Henry Kissinger began secret peace talks in Paris. In 1972 Nixon was re-elected with the promise of "a secret plan to end the war" and the inept anti-war campaign of George McGovern. Nixon's secret squad of "plumbers" were caught breaking into Democratic headquarters at the Watergate, begin-ning the unraveling of Tricky Dick. 1973 brought the end of the draft, the release of 590 American POW's, further withdrawal and limiting of U.S. combat troops. South Vietnamese armed forces totalled 1,110,000 (223,748 KIA's). In August 1974 Nixon avoided impeachment by resigning. In 1975 the NVA captured Hue, Danang and Saigon – End of war; April 30, 1975 –

U.S. war dead: 58,000 (all of whose names would be carved into a black granite wall

in Washington, D.C.)

Enemy losses: 3,600,000 (no wall).

(2000)

# ALL GOOD

I turned on the tube
just to watch the pols bob and weave.
I swear to god, darlin' –
I never thought that you'd leave.
Daddy came home from his war a hero.
The best we got from ours was zero.
When I was young I bragged.
"You know I'm good at travelling light –
Light's all I've got
and I'm trying to shed that."
The Laureate entered –
a tenured professor in a necktie.
(never trust a used car salesman
wearing bluejeans).
The eighty year old poet
finally finished his only epic
and sighed some mild relief –
Lonelier than a hermit's funeral.
The Minister for Rapid Exhaustion
of Non-Renewable Resources
pronounced time a one-way street.
The Secretary of Commercial Exploitation
leapt to his feet with applause.
"All I know is what I read in the newspapers"

is a long way from
"I believe what I see on TV" –
where only the prettiest faces
bring us the ugliest news.


They're selling death and gasolene.
We're paying taxes for their wars.
We may have overstayed our welcome:
Overconsuming and living too long.
Out in the burbdocks:
Cyberscum, techno-creeps
clogging up the lanes
Ad-mad and fantasy foolish –
Down on the corporate farm
there is no pony just for riding.
Old people in the supermarket
are poking packages of meat,
as if to test the feeling of dead flesh.
Do I hear "crumble-down economics"?
Or maybe its just one of those mornings,
I stumble to work
not particularly proud of my species.
A bald woman keeps walking in and out of the room
in search of her eyebrows.
Now the birds conspire against us
with viruses to arrest our unchecked reign.
They fly in the face of arrogance.

    Do you think this microbial dance is happen-
stance?
   Out on a cold winter sidewalk
     a man huddled over his cigarette,
       wearing a salon tan,
         is arguing over a cell phone
           with his soon-to-be-ex-wife
             over   custody   of   the   frozen
embryos.
   All of the niche marketers
     are lined up in the mall
         like an econo-firing squad.
  Now its May in January
   And December in April.
     she was trying to make the scene
       when there wasn't one left
         (whales are committing suicide
           as we fill the oceans with carbon
dioxide).
   Sure,
  we'll pretend to be emperor
     though we've not a stitch on,
       walking through the Middle East
         where all must be covered.

                       (2004)

# REMNANTS AND PENANCE

As-Salámn 'Alaykum
    (Peace be unto you)


The deluded versus the excluded –
  our overpaid Hessians
    battle their paradise-bound martyrs.
  Our warriors ride into the fray
      blaring heavy metal goth rock (death of the
cool).
      God save us or damn us.


I remember when "the movement"
    was always in the background music
    and spring was in my step.
  Now a surgeon has removed my swagger
    and a shrink suppressed my palaver,
      while madmen rule the country yet
    and corn that could be fed to the world's starving
      feeds our insatiable engines instead.


I go to drop my last dime
    into a pay phone

                              (to call her)

                    and it says,

                              "50 cents now brother –

                                   ain't you got no cell?"


Late for the shape-shifters' convention,
   now I'm wandering empty streets so lost.
      Smile in the sunshine feels good.
         At ten below I start feeding

                              stray cats in the alley.
               where is the new rebel?
                  There must be a new rebel. . . . .
                     we surely can't settle
                        for this kettle empty of fish.


The president starts awake in a cold night sweat
   at the globalized industrialman-made
         mass species extinction underway in his rule.
            (only a zoo-ful of DNA on file
                  and a seedbank account underground.)
   Two wings of one political party
      offer a fork in the road
                  that leads back to a merger –
         The illusion of choice to sustain us:
            This modern twitch,
               This imperial itch.

well-oiled Washington
blood-blinded in Babylon.


wa' Alaikum As-Salám
(And peace be unto you).


(2007)

Part Two:

## THE NANCY POEMS

"Don't you start me talkin',
I'll tell everything I know."

- Sonny Boy Williamson

# THE NANCY POEMS

1. Woman (1975)
2. Love Is A Velvet Chain (1981)
3. Without Progress (1987)
4. Black Crow Blues (1988)
5. Reunion (1991)
6. Pastorale Past (1991)
7. Poetic Justice (1992)
8. Past Voice Present (2001)
9. On Calling An Old Flame (2007)

# WOMAN

In this age of storms
    you are servant of the wind
        and I,
                the vassal of thunder.
You are as the wheel of turning seasons –
    your colors shift
        and your shapes are melting.
           I am the rain of the morning,
                You are the vessel of evening –
    we are dissolving into a starswirl
        of sweet light
            sleeping on the tongue of the dreamer.
I can feel the forms changing now;
    the names are all reordered –
        Speaking your true name
                    scatters the demons of doubt
And
    you must be the pool of endless depth;
        I must be the stone of constant dropping.

(1975)

Philip Finkle

# LOVE IS A VELVET CHAIN

On the journey to the markets
  we've met at the crossroads of cunning
    and there lies a velvet chain.
      And among the oaks and sycamores,
        along the ridge of pines –
    You are a forest
          full of wild things,
      And I am a blundering pioneer.

There are wrens and robins;
  there are moles and squirrels
    and hawks and crayfish
      and catfish and barley,
        milkweed and daisies
      and the names are myriad.
        (You,
           the ocean of memory;
      I,
          the molecule of desire.)

I've wandered from the road to ruin;
  our eyes have met

on a narrow path
    through clover and foxtail
        and ants and bees
    and a cast of hawks
        circling high
                overhead.
woman is possibility.
    man is expectation.

(1981)

# WITHOUT PROGRESS

There is no season for love, my love;
  There is no reason for time –
    There is a rhythym that binds us here,
        though yours may not be mine.
      Prayers may not be answered now;
          Fortunes entangle, untwine.

Autumn dogs summer
    as you, constant, stalk my heart.
  Keepers and sleepers arise for the call:
      This temporary stage is mine.
    It's a slow, slow dance we're doing, love,
        in this short, short span we stride.

You've been teaching bingo strategy to the very confused;
  I paint teardrops on the faces on postage stamps –
    There are innumerable ways to skin a cat,
        but practically none to like it.

I have learned to sleep with my hands in my pockets.
You have learned to live with your heart in a locket.

(1987)

# BLACK CROW BLUES

Black crow, red sun.
  Begin as two, end as one.

I remember your lace curtains,
  I believed your lying eyes.
I felt you always there beside me.
  I woke up inside your sighs.
        I don't know if I've been cheated,
            I don't care if I've been blind.
        I just want to hear your laughter
            echo down the walls of time.

Grey sky, brown ground.
  Rain falls with vegetal sound.

I can't forget the lips you had then,
  I can't remember what words they said.
I never knew where your gypsy wants led.
  We're all just becoming "has-beens"
                right up to the moment that we end.
  I don't care which way the creek flows,
      I've punched my ticket to the end.

I only know what the phoebe tells me:
There's true religion 'round the bend!


Loving thighs, nurturing breasts.
I'm a question, you're the quest.


You put a candle in the window,
when I was no more than a thief.
when I was thirsty without water,
You offered me relief.
My mind's at the cleaner's, my soul's a misdemeanor.
Your heart's now surrounded by a fence of finest
mesh.
I may have trashed all your wordy goodlies
till they weren't worth a lousy
dime.
But I always cherished your perishing flesh.


Morning thrush, evening swallow.
Night falls, day follows.

(1988)

46

# REUNION

It's the Full Grass Moon
    and we're mired here in maya –
Now the subtle rains begin.
    I'm trying to read the signs.
        They say timing is crucial –
    With you, my timing is simple,

                is always.
The Pink Flower Moon illumines the face
        of *mi compañera* of True North.
        we discuss the world of dust.
          Together we are celebation:
            The stranger who loves
like kin,

             the fire that we
might have been!
    From opposite banks of the river we wave;
      You with an Ace,
        And I but a knave.
    we've each been the meal that predators crave.
      (We've all been foolish
          and a few of us brave.)

Dragons won't come when you summon
And you can't hear the songs that bats sing.
The future is where dreams live
(to the present they flock)
The past is a graveyard of dreams

it seems.

Parts of the imaginary and parts of the real
are not visible to you.

And parts are.

May we stay alive long enough
to be

what we

might have been.

(1991)

# PASTORLAE PAST

Queen Anne's lace and chicory
        line the road to our past history.
  There is wonder all around –
         we mistake it for just ground.
  You're high-strung and I'm low-key.
      we were never sure just what to do.
  You spoiled me for anyone else,
        And I ruined me for you.
  In daylight we sketched smoky schemes,
       By night we searched each other's seams:
    scars left by bad gambles, revolving losses with no
handles.
  I looked deep into your eyes
       and thought I saw us: destiny.
  I watched you turn and walk away
        and learned synchronicity.
   Ever since the crash it's been no fun.
  After all these years I'm quite good at one.
  We're older now, it won't be long.
    Cicadas' pulse anchors the song;
      Crickets' licks join in the tune:

Philip Finkle

The insect world jams with the moon.
I'm the one on whom you can depend –
where does the wind start?
where does time end?
I can't remember my dreams.
I can't forget your face.
we walked through chicory and Queen Anne's lace.

(1991)

# POETIC JUSTICE

Let the many become the few,
  Now its another turndown day
      Here in the land of the brew and the home of the
fey –
          The battle of poets is not visionary.
              It is academic.
          Archivists of anger, on the cusp,
                  soon to be dust,
              How many-thorned thy rose?
  we know all of the old stories;
      we crave the undomesticated new –
          we have muddy thoughts and lots of isms.
          we have little hope and many prisons.
  Won't you please tell me, Pilot –
      are we heavenbound or forlorn?
  why do we keep settling for the least possible world?
      Have we lost the sidereal rhythym to our flesh-
driven rhyme?
  I met a fire with her eyes,
      I've never known those ties that bind,
          I recognize neither you nor your disguise.
          we're each so human and no one's pure.

Life's so short and nothing's sure.

It's true there was a woman once.

Her heart was wide and her mind was lean.

I might have been the longest shot in town;

She was the best thing I'd ever seen.

She still had good luck charms and daydreams;

I didn't seem to fit in anywhere.

I wove poverty grass and larkspur

into a wreath that she refused to wear in

her hair.

(1992)

# PAST VOICE PRESENT

It was the Crow Moon when you called.
  winter's grip had just loosened.
         so much of love consists of lost causes.
    Now its the Year of the Horse again
             (twice since we were together).
         Perhaps modern love is just
                 the desire for what cannot be –
         Ideas (wishes for the impossible)
                 chasing actual flesh.


I am an old man now,
    with no mother and no child.
  I can't keep from crying in the movies –
             sometimes I remember to kneel
                 but forget how to pray.
         Sleep is a foreign country
                 in which I cannot stay long.
         Count me in or count me out.
             Help me sing or let me shout.
All of the so-called adults
  are eating milkduds and watching vampire movies.

Philip Finkle

Alone is not the same as lonely –
But I wish I could lie
once again in your arms.

(2001)

# ON CALLING ON OLD FLAME

You had the full fire then –
  where has that flame now gone?
    Are you sheltering the spark inside?
    Are you searching for the ark?
      The machinery's breakin' down
                all around us and within.
          we,
                once young, lean, so hungry;
                      now sated and dim.
                Been that, done there;
                seen where, begat naught.
          Keep the chatter short,
                let the verse go long –
    Make the coffee and the women strong,
        Serve the tea too hot and the beer too cold,
                My friends still young when old.
          Delivery first, promises last.
          Kisses slow, true words never past.
                Laughter easy, hatred hard –
        Expect by the inch, forgive by the yard.
  I remember the smile in your eyes

and the light on your lips,

that laser beam look

and that saber sharp wit.

what's the skinny on the pall?

what free bear still awes us all?

Rain till it floods, drought till its bones –

Brother Frog, Sister Swallow so long.

The real never ending, life bringing grief.

The gift of clear reason,

the pure sigh of relief.

I was crazy too often.

You've been distant too long.

I've been solved as a cipher.

You will seem as a song.

(2007)

Part Three:

## PASTS AND REPASTS

"Who setting forth encounters himself
has been the world journey."

- Kenneth Patchen

# PASTS AND REPASTS

1. In Her Memory (1995)
2. Rocky Trip (2001)
3. Survivoyage (2008)
4. Hoperise (2008)
5. Maggie's Blues (2009)
6. Prophesy (2009)
7. The Turning (2010)
8. Creed (2010)
9. For A Distant Cohort (2012)
10. Reprieve Again (2013)
11. Preamble To A Gamble (2013)
12. Last Curse Of Pestilence (A Love Song) (2013)
13. Mortality (2014)
14. Ancestrale (2014)
15. Generic Engineering (2014)
16. Playing By Dozens (2014)
17. Manifesto (2015)

# IN HER MOMERY

- for Phyllis June Finkle
(1918 - 1995)

She told me that if you throw mud
   you're bound to get some on yourself.
     But I was young and angry -
      And I did.

Her pastor called her an ambassador of faith.
    ("It doesn't matter if you understand it completely,
       but only that you practice it.")
Some will say that she's gone to a better place;
   I only know that every place she ever was,
      was made better by her presence.
Found among her writings:
   "If you worry about it,
     you draw it to you."
   And:
    "Envy likes to talk."

Redbud blooms blaze her color each year.
   This is the time Native Americans called:
     "The Moon of Little Frogs Croaking."
      Life is renewing.
        The ducks soon arrive in variously-colored bibs.
       The truly cruelest month has come,
        And our kindest one is gone.

- 1995

Philip Finkle

# ROCKY TRIP

In Victor, Colorado we came upon a mountain
    actually being raped - torn down and dragged
    through cyanide pits to leach out all of the gold.
Ouray and Chipeta had lived in a white-man-house
    and gone to Washington often to talk to politicians
    and bureaucrats about adapting to white man ways.
The Colorado Gold Rush of 1859 led to a drastic
    reduction of the Ute population - from 8,000
    to 2,000 in 20 years.
And now there are many fewer Blue Sky People and
    and more powerful mining interests and methods.


North of the Arkansas River,
    Up along Eight-Mile Creek
      Through Phantom Canyon,
        dodging cattle in the road -
We drove up the Front Range to camp at Thunder Ridge,
                          near Rampart Reservoir.
    In the morning Hunga fired up the camp stove
      to cook his usual campers' breakfast:
        bacon, eggs, and pancakes:
          "It don't get no better!"
Snow flurries started
    so we sat in the back of the truck to eat.
Later that day we hightailed it for Guanella Pass
    but it was closed by the snow -

So we backtracked to Evergreen
   where we hopped onto the Interstate -
Cars were off in the ditch right and left.
We drove on to Idaho Springs -
   When neither Dan'l nor the Mrs. were at the B.P.O.E. -
      we called ahead
        "Here we come!
     Up Fall River Road,
      never slowing down,
    We sped up to Hamlin Gulch
   Right to the front door of the house
     that Dan had built in the mountains.
  We talked late into the night
        with Dan and Sharon
      while skies cleared
   and Hunga demonstrated another of his survival skills,
      earning a new nickname.
    Sharon christened him "Fire Guy".
Warm and safe we unrolled our sleeping bags
    under skylight windows
      looking out on many more stars than we had
            back home in Missouri.
Gazing around the next morning,
  Fire Guy announced,
    "Wow!
      - every window is a postcard!"

                 - 2001

Philip Finkle

# SURVIVOYAGE

"If I don't go crazy baby -
I swear I'm gonna lose my mind."
- Otis Spahn

Now too old to go out in a blaze of glory,
Yet too young to depart without telling the story -
The conventional wisdom is nine parts convention
and one part wisdom.
Here the status pros
are all status quos,
wearing corporate logos on their souls.
Here where counter-revoltionaries really count
and revolutions go to burn out:
the pols promise we can have it all
without the pall
that we can feel fast approaching
the despair encroaching.
Love is blind;
sometimes deaf, dumb and stupid too.
It's nothing new
that so much of history is hormones.
Beware smart bombs and blinkered leaders,
high rollers and bottom-feeders.
What will survive is a riddle -
Hey diddle, diddle;
Species burn while
sapiens fiddles.

Ice to fire,
Lightning to thunder,
Humble rise above,
Arrogant sink under.
Life to the worthy
Death to pretenders -
When will we tire of rule by the true dead-enders?
Where now are the Mississippi sturgeon that my father loved?
There were mussel shells to turn into Iowa buttons
more marvelous than petro-plastics..
Corn was food for folks,
not fuel for fools.
Those who can't tell flame from from tools
wil end with hands of ashes.
The material mind
misses the departing dream.
All board now,
there's a train that's leaving.
Wave good-bye
to that gang deceiving.
They own the station,
We're down the line receding.
There's a journey to be cherished.
There's reason to relish.
There's anguish to spare and hubris to burn.
Equilibrium grows from the bottom up.
Domination tumbles from the top to disaster.

- 2008

# HOPERISE

It's near midnight darlin' -
    All of the swine are begging for pearls:
      "My throne for a pork chop, my whine for a thrill -
        Sing just one song recalling my name,
          Illumine my dream, spark my flame -
          Extinguish hate, prime desire."
Where's the princess when the Queen is dead?
    Why is the King always out of his head?
      It's now night in the Kingdom,
        Praise dawn should she rise.
        Death is the question, life is the prize.
      While there are fish in the ocean and birds in the air
      There's still hope in the alley and a cure for despair.
Play patriarch, play brazen bitch.
    No matter where, no matter which -
      Ms. God will calm your yaw, will scratch your itch.
        Ring true in timbre, sound pure of pitch:
    No matter we're the short of the long.
      Every felt note part of a greater song -
        The balance of the great design,
          If we don't fit the scheme then we shall fall.
It's the new global economy:
    Dwindling blue fin, seabass and swordfish
            rounded up in a dance of disappearance.
    From the South
          uncut cocaine by air, land or sea,
           fresh-cut flowers by overnight air;

Tech support from India;
Sex-slave franchises available worldwide;
Giant machines and gruntwork shipped to China
while Sinica Pax, Inc. opens American wind machine and
solar panel factories.
Is it the end of the anthropocene
or the Kali Yuga?
Children of forced serial rape,
Children stolen from the soon-to-be-disappeared,
Children forced to be warriors.
Organ scavengers haunting nightstreets
in search of youthful eyes and kidneys.
The Childrens' Goddess drifts in as a blue mist.
She feels like a hurt that's been kissed.
Aleha is a name they call her.
The Oneness is another.
There's a profligate priest and a reverend of could;
A pope of repentance, an imam of would.
"I Am the Great I Was, I Will Be the Greater She."
I believe every true love is part of a greater love -
every pure song sung in a dharmic voice:
The ordinary deluxe,
Pachamama redux!

- 2008

Philip Finkle

# MAGGIE'S BLUES

- for Mary Beth

She said call me Sadie,
        though that was not her name.
    When she was young the bowl never emptied
                and the glass always refilled.
        She smoked weed like Louis Armstrong
                and made love like Miss Monroe.
        She seemed a soul shot full of holes too soon -
        Desire for love sprang eternal and blind
                just like pushing on a string.
She said call me Zelda,
    That's who I feel I must be.
    She burned the middle from both ends.
        Its easier to repeat the past
        than to live with a fortune-teller -
        She'd tried both and more,
            she repented nothing.
        She risked her future for a song.
        She just laughed when things went wrong,
            said, "I knew it all along."
            "God promised me nothing," she said,
                "and delivered on Her word."

You've got to take the sweet where you find it,
    endure the bitter most the time.
  Cats curled all around her,
    Old blues tunes stoked her flame.
While I wondered when she might come home
   She'd found an attic with a view
    in the home of an outlaw for free.
  Who knows what she saw in the thief
    that she couldn't find in me.
Years have rolled by,
  she's in the ether now:
  Either up or down, in the chips or not.
    I never knew what she really wanted
      But I do know what she got.

- 2009

# PROPHECY

Lost souls wandering parking lots and job fairs
   hear the humming of the dynamos of destruction.
  They've slaughtered the lamb,
     Now the rooster has fled.
    Can't touch your heart, they'll get into your head.
      The fat man is speaking, the prophet's now mum.
      The most uncertain shout loudest;
        doctor give me a shot.
     Who'll announce the dawn when the light's gone out?
      Don't take your gun to town,
        its a hotbed of deceit.
     What looks like victory
         is most certainly defeat.
     We're all born to die -
       Pour another one, sister -
      There's despair all around.
 The past seems to make no sense
   when the future runs aground.
Dreams of autumn are the sweetest, treading on frost.

Hopes of clarity arise from schemes lost,
She lay next to me, I couldn't speak -
Her presence strong, my words so weak.
She had just a thin coat for winter.
I slept only with a sheet.
I've been crazy and I've been sane.
Sometimes I know the difference,
Sometimes they seem just the same.
Which is truer depends on the time
Just as the circle grows from the line.
Oracle bones and ancient coins -
misfortune beckons:
Blasphemy and irreverance rule the day.
Because you can doesn't mean that you should.
If there is no will there can be no would.
Increase precedes decline.
Decrease prepares arise.

- 2009

Philip Finkle

# THE TURNING

So far along this cursed road,
   relentless rains pour down.
     Adharma abounds:
       Another foul spill in the ocean
         and still a hole in the sky.
     The Sixth Great Extinction is underway
        and I still can't find the gypsy.
      The president strokes a bewitching fiddle
         while senators idly watch the empire burn.
    I'd like to find an old dog;
     Have him teach me a new trick.
    I'd like a new companion
     who knows all of my old licks.
   The way the wind blows
     and the ways the the rivers flow -
      These are restless times:
    Not so hard to judge the way to go
      as it is to follow what you know.
Again she's taken a new lover.
   I'm accumulating more dead friends.
  Seasons go quickly,
   reason grows slowly.
    Time passes by on the way to "too late".

Eco-disassociative disorders rule the day.
    I'm ranting at the TV news:
       armageddon militias
          and hate-blind pundatriots.
    Megawatts and yottabytes
      command with seductive call of ease:
       sweet as suicide, distant as love -
       Unable to pull ourselves out of the muck
       we're left to pray for blind luck.
  The oil-sick bastards always get their money back.
    It's only justice that we lack.
  The digitals entail strict parameters,
    as with wooly mammoth certitude
    we stomp on to resolution.
    Only property confers rank,
      Wealth the only source of devotion.
   Only lust bonds the sexes.
    Commercial order drives legation.
The destruction of inequities mirrors
  the waiting demise of Ur -
So a new beginning may emerge.
  Again the wheel revealed.

                 - 2010

# CREED

Practice patience.
Promote harmony.
Despise greed.
Admire beauty.
Avoid malice.
Respect nature.
Contribute balance.
Embrace humility.
Scorn pride.
Disparage extravagance.
Celebrate wonder.
Stay vigilant.
Speak truth.

- 2010

# FOR A DISTANT COHORT

- for Mike Brewer, Ashland Poet

Another Super Nova
    signalled from near Ursa Major.
- He counted to One:
        the Universe in a mere grain.
    Pondering stars
      he drew charts.
    Searching the Order
      he threw hexagrams.
    Still mystery lingered
     while he worried his beads.
   He drove the djinn
      from the dark forest.
   His needs were minimal.
    He maximized his deeds.
The fewest words
    were the most adequate gift,
     The least gesture
    the final lift.
   Shape-changing -
    web-footed on broken water.
     As a cold vow
      we grow old now -
    And finally the snow.
    Hold him,
      let him go.

- 2012

Philip Finkle

# REPRIEVE AGAIN

for Nancy

Your chaste kiss hails winter's end.
   Your sure eyes still kindle hope -
     the years fall away
         like tears astray.
    We laugh, we sigh,
       though death grows nigh.
     We stroll through graveyards ever growing,
       Whistling past tombstones
         of old friends and lovers
           dressed in their graduation gowns
          long past mind and body
         now spirits soar.

Things looked grim to her.
   She was feeling mishandled and disgruntled.
     "Where's the fairy tale ending
       when you really need it?"
     "Can't we waltz around the room once more?"
         I thought.

Lookin' for a new deal
>> at another crossroads
>>> with the same old Devil.
> I stepped behind a tree
>> just long enough to commit poetry.
>> The times were different then
>>> as were we.
> Happy songs leave the devil cold.
>> Why go down without a fight?
>> We can at least leave
>>> our footprints in the sand.

Samizdat from Mayakovsky:
> Poetry can be drawn only from the future
>> and not from the past,

— 2013

Philip Finkle

# PREAMBLE TO A GAMBLE

Just outside of the shuck and thrive
    its jive and drive
    and contrails in the sky
        spelling heat death -
   Collapsing ice shelves,
      melting permafrost.
   Constant running air-conditioning
     to cool megadatacenterservers.
   The elite in their palatial, climate-controlled perches
        with panoramic views.
  Fracking on the fault lines,
   apparatchiks of avarice abound.
   Necropolis, D.C. signals.)
    (No parliament of owls here.)
  Canaries screaming bloody murder from the mines.
   Seems like endtimes
    but its just the end of innocence.
 Petro-cowboys and their steadfast whores
   party on at Fort McMurray
      and the Bakken....
Prophet just one day ahead of the doom.
    Drugs and high-octane daydreams:
    Race to annihilation
      yields exhiliration.
  Put on your tinfoil hat
    and bring a child into this world.
  We're losing cards in a hand
     on a sinking ship.
Children, you must be better than us
    or we're just ashes and dust.

- 2013

# LAST CURSE OF PESTILENCE
# (A LOVE SONG)

Back in the day,
when there was still a Way,
¿Sabe?
Waitin' for the Ufty McGufty -
Ziggurat of Arrogance toppled like a house of cards.
We once ruled the Kingdom and then blew it;
baked a bisquit but could not chew it.
Prosperity Gospel:
a blind man can see your point -
A white man could lead your band.
"Pioneers get the arrows,
the settlers get the land."
Great Lakes not so great these days.
They'll overflow when the ice in my drink melts -
Asian carp up the Mississippi.
I need an appointment to talk with the Shaman.
"Nam myoho renge kyo"

There are plastic islands in the Ocean.
Evil and Greed are loose in the World.
Trains and ocean freighters are the price
Earth must bear for us.
But its a sea change comin', Buster.
Mighty airline moguls fly high enough
to poke a finger in God's eye.
Popes in Fords lookin' for Honky Tonk Jesus.
Assassins on motorbikes,
martyrs with exploding trucks
and automatic weapons.

Philip Finkle

Pull over, Cowboy!
    Don't go off that cliff.
    Old Silk Road brings rails bearing gifts.
    Enough for all to sip.
            Don't gulp, pup -
There are only so many teats to suck.
        Some will swim, some will sink.
            "Nam myoho renge kyo"

Lord knows I'm no saint:
        Somethings I can, somethings I can't.
I was a soldier for the Empire.
    Is this my reward?
  To witness the last weary stages of a decayed, self-consuming
        techno-military-industrial-capitalism.
        "Have your contractors talk to my people;
            I'm sure we can do business."
    You be Bonnie and I'll be Clyde
        though I'm not yet drunk enough to watch the evening news.
            We've already tipped at the point.
    I was at the top of my game, she couldn't remember my name -
        anarcho-prophet or profiteer?
    Though I am a son of the Mother of Waters,
        Pasts are futures that didn't last
            and its way past Dawn.
    The privileged will not give up their privileges
                            without a struggle
        and not a moment too soon
                    some will sink and some will swim.
            "Nam myoho renge kyo"

80

Full circle now, I'm staring into space -
    sometimes feeling a disgrace
                to some race from which I must resign.
    You got your signals crossed, your children lost -
      Progeny recapitulates pathology.
         (who gets a bigger chunk of the cinder?)
Thesis, antithesis, synthesis.
    Life is desire, Desire leads to suffering.
    Brahma, Shiva, Vishnu.
 Dressed mostly in feathers,
        she had many levers.
    I had barely a grip on things - I needed her lift.
    Information, disinformation, interpretation.
    The Moon, she swings from side to side
            again, again
              later and later.
    Creation, destruction, preservation.
      He said to turn the other cheek but we only have two.
      No more, no better.
La Niña, el niño, nada:
    the Earth is as beautiful or as hideous
          as we paint her with our lives.
           ("Thanks, I'll have another.")
    You have more colors than I have rhymes.
    You always paint outside my lines.
    "Nam myoho renge kyo."

                            - 2013

Philip Finkle

# MORTALITY

I can swear.
    I can lie.
        There's no mistake - I'm clay.
  I gave in to my rage.
    I tore out a page,
                or two,
                    or three.
I am Lord of the Interstate:
        A menace to the innocents who live along the way.


A Gypsy Jew with a Mustang blew through town,
           stole our Mary Lou.
       Now its your worst nightmare
              in a baby carriage.
  Dude threw a cymbal on the floor.
  An English chased some symbol out the door.
Its one thing to run with horses,
        another with the buffalo.
  I hate to say I told you so.
    I still crave the flesh
        but consult the bones.
  Some one said, "Words without action are hollow;
        Actions without words are blind."

The gods gave us wine for a reason,
They gave us sorrows for each season.
We chased the herds till they thinned.
Then so did we.
Your latest idol showin' feet of clay.
The richest man in the world has his velvet slipper
on my throat.
His jackbooted jackals mine our ore,
drill our oil,
suck the marrow from our bones,
Bleed the rain from our forest.
A Silver Dagger and a Golden Throne
now reduced to dust.
Death is a dune.

- 2014

Philip Finkle

# ANCESTRALE

I, poet manqué,
    goin' down slow.
      I'll bet these and hold 'em,
          hopin' for one last show,
            just limpin' to the finish line -
       Emboldened by the wild ones
                    still among us here.
    There is a giant metal bird of presumption
          that we fly for granted to destruction.
    There is barely time enough
        to turn our ship from the cliff of the sea.

One of the Old Ones fed squirrels from his hand
              and had a Bible hard as stone.
    He worked the trains
        and he was maimed
          but came back stronger.
  Then a bad seed infected his eldest daughter:
      the grandfather I never knew -
       A Magnificent Tenor,
       A Master Plumber;
            A drunkard and a womanizer.
      He seemed exciting, remote and disturbing.
       Grandma was resourceful and forgiving.
  Ain't no pain that someone isn't singing about.
  Once more I've bitten off more than I can chew.

I, heirophant of the mysteries,
kykeon imbiber
stared straight into the fire
like Bill the Welder.
Another Elder smoked cigars
and even sometimes wore suspenders.
He outran flood and drought
And after the fall of Jerusalem,
the Crusades, the Inquisition,
the pogroms, the camps, the ovens -
Now you wanna draw down, hombre?
On me, Manu, Hoss and Little Lev?
Enough's enough;
not 'nuf, not 'nuf.
Go for it, cousin.
We feast together or we hunger.
Carnal craves the eternal
But we'll be finished sooner or later
by fire or the ruins of desire.
Now cult célèbre is ordináire.
Naked Desire or Lethal Hate,
With no solution, here we wait.

- 2014

# GENERIC ENGINEERING

"The United States is the great unspanked baby of the world."
- John French Sloan

Who you callin' invasive, Invader?
  Its Our Oligarchs vs. Their Oligarchs.
   The Know-Nots are only too willing to rule.
    If you make war on Earth she will defeat you.
   Can you show us how to build a fast machine?
    How about a breed to last:
       lean and fleet afoot from start to past -
        a little bit crazy but a whole lot of kind.


  We're not done yet
    but we can see it from here.
   We'll quit swimming soon;
     the shore is near.
    You need not be a prophet to spy catatrophe ahead.
    The troubadors are troubled now.
      Their songs do not end well.
   Who are you to judge?
   New Rebel Priest
     we pray.
  One thing's for sure:
   there are many more ways to be certain
       than to be right.
We put marks on sticks before we could speak.
 We're all bizarre sometimes.
  History is longer than time.
  Time is shorter than us.
It's all over in an instant -
  You tend the flock, brother.

I know the way North.
Perhaps we'll survive The Deluge.
We knew less than we thought.
We know more than we ought.
I know there should be more to see.
This can't be the end of we.
Who knew that you were planning a pirate voyage?
Don't let them play you for a chump, chump.
Let's not end just an oil slick in the sea.
I'm going nowhere till the grave, girl.
I'll be waiting for the Wave and you, ma'am
here near the swirling exit.
Pangaia is a hope.
Silence that knows the Way
is the wisest thing that we can say.
Oh my plump silly countrymen:
Suck it up. Stop fuckin' up.
What flies must come to rest on Earth.
We set off with some Bolivians to see the Glacier,
but when we arrived there was no glacier there.
Oh, the finch,
oh, the sparrow -
The way once wide now made so narrow.
A hawk came down from the river
to see what there was to hunt.
Now no one's hands are clean:
stained with blood and pollen.
Our modern breath drenched in pesticides and pestilence.
We'll just fiddle with your jeans:
A little altering of genes.
When the bee and butterfly are gone
we can't be far behind.

- 2014

Philip Finkle

# PLAYING BY DOZENS

It's not hard to be a hermit
              when your last friend's gone.
   After twelve tribes dispersed,
    Back when I was just a ghost,
      Always a sucker for some Mary,
       Swimming in deep water,
          never breathing pure ether,
  I made the most of my adventures -
    There weren't that many:
      there never are.
        We're here; we're over.
Twelve houses of the zodiac revolve
            as we dissolve.
  We need the order of the free.
   She tasted of honey and chaos:
      Pretty Baby struts her stuff in some arena.
        Meanwhile our hopes are growin' leaner.
Shop-lifting Chinese shoes is its own punishment.
  All my dreams are tamed and shackled.
   We know what we're up against,
            still Caesar.
    Honest work is hard to find
          in the Kingdom of the Few.
  When you're rich, you make your own rules.
   When you're poor with nothing to lose,
         then you can too.

At all 12 gates to the City
    Carny Angels give out good medicine to any stranger
                         (the stranger the better).
  I say, why be a poet,
        if you don't use the license?
   I'm tired of pullin' the plow.
     Now's time for reapin'.
No more war stories please.
   Best be strong and steady:
       slow to anger,
              quick to reply.
  There was a faulty imam
          in the chain of succession.
       Now it's a Caliphate of cupidity and cruelty
         (not what we'd hoped for)..
Backs to the wall,
   Where go we now?
  12 apostles have spoken.
  All of their words have been broken.
 Waters risin':
    Last Desperate Attempt
      to cleanse Earth's curse from memory.
       Be it We?

                     - 2014

# MANIFESTO

Waiting for the world mind
    whose every action is a pebble in the pond
    and also all of the resulting ripples.
When you walk your dog in a civilized city
    you're obliged to pick up after it
    But when the privileged fly
    they leave detritus in the sky.
As the special few flit around the globe like there's no tomorrow,
    perhaps they're right.
    They're off New York to L.A.,
    To London, Frankfurt and Davos,
    Dubai, Mumbai and Cairo,
    Istanbul, Moscow and Sydney,
    Toronto, Shanghai and Rio,
    Johannesburg, Hong Kong and Cartagena.
Besides jet fuel for the few
    the Satanic Mills still burn coal
    (Powder River Basin and Galilee Basin yet to be exhausted)
    and oil is black gold to be squandered.

Now fossil fuels are not enough.
    Rare earth elements are commodities for consumption.
      Bolivia's lithium is alluring.
         Coltan is needed for mobile electronic devices
              so its mined in remote jungles of the Congo
            where weary miners are fed bushmeat
                    until the mountain gorillas run out.
There's more than enough techno-titillation
            to distract us from survival quandries.
    Its just another day at the kleptocratic office:
    The hive mind wields its algorithms in quest of mastery.
Venture communism or vulture capitalism:
        who's the hegemon now?
  So we kick the can down the road
            waiting for the world mind to evolve
               and deal with the truth and its consequences.

                        (2015)